BABY ELEPHANT

Published in Canada by Fitzhenry & Whiteside, 195 Allstate Parkway, Markham, Ontario L3R 4T8

Published in the United States by Fitzhenry & Whiteside, 121 Harvard Avenue, Suite 2, Allston, Massachusetts 02134

10 9 8 7 6 5 4 3 2 1

National Library of Canada Cataloguing in Publication Data
Lang, Aubrey
Baby elephant / text by Aubrey Lang ; photography by Wayne Lynch.

(Nature babies)
ISBN 1-55041-715-0 (bound).--ISBN 1-55041-717-7 (pbk.)

1. Elephants--Infancy--Juvenile literature. I. Lynch, Wayne II. Title. III. Series.

QL737.P98L34 2002   j599.67'139   C2002-901612-6

U.S. Cataloging-in-Publication Data
(Library of Congress Standards)

Lang, Aubrey.
Baby elephant / text by Aubrey Lang ; photography by Wayne Lynch. -- 1st ed.
[32] p. : col. photos. ; cm.   (Nature babies)
Summary: No one is more important to the baby elephant than its mother. But there are other members of the extended family who will care for and protect this little one from harm. Under their vigilant watch, the baby elephant can grow and discover the world.
ISBN 1-55041-715-0
ISBN 1-55041-717-7 (pbk.)
1.Elephants -- Juvenile literature. [1. Elephants.] I. Lynch, Wayne, 1948- . II. Title. III. Series.
599.64 [E] 21   2002   CIP

Fitzhenry & Whiteside acknowledges with thanks the Canada Council for the Arts, the Government of Canada through the Book Publishing Industry Development Program (BPIDP), and the Ontario Arts Council for their support for our publishing program.

Design by Wycliffe Smith
Printed in Hong Kong

BABY ELEPHANT

Text by Aubrey Lang
Photography by Wayne Lynch

Fitzhenry & Whiteside

BEFORE YOU BEGIN

Dear Reader,

We love to watch and photograph wild animals. Sometimes they make us happy; sometimes they make us sad. We wrote this book to share with you some of the adventures in the life of a baby elephant. It is exciting to photograph animals in wild places, and we are always careful not to harm or upset them.

To photograph the elephants in this book, we spent many weeks living in East Africa and following the family in a little car that was much smaller than a mother elephant.

This book is dedicated to Renée, whose warmth and encouragement we cherish.

— Aubrey Lang and Wayne Lynch

TABLE OF CONTENTS

Before You Begin	4
A Bumpy Start	8
Meet the Family	10
Grandmother in Charge	12
Busy Bulls	14
Caring for Baby	16
Trunk Practice	20
Mud Bath	22
Older and Braver	24
On the Move	28
Help Me Up!	30
Here to Stay	32
Did You Know?	34
Index	35
Biographies	36

It is the end of the rainy season on the Serengeti Plains of East Africa. Zebras, gazelles, and herds of wildebeest graze on juicy green grasses. Noisy hippos soak in the muddy rivers. Golden lions snooze in the sunshine, and giraffes as tall as houses nibble on the trees.

Many elephant families also live here, and today the Kichwa Tembo family is more excited than usual.

A few days ago a new fuzzyheaded baby female joined the family. Her mother was standing when she gave birth, and the baby landed on the ground with a thud. Within hours she was strong enough to wobble behind her mother's bristly tail.

The elephant is the largest land animal in the world, and this baby girl was a whopper. At birth, she weighed more than an adult man.

The baby elephant lives in a family that includes her mother, her brothers and sisters, several aunts and cousins, and her grandmother. With twenty members, this elephant family is larger than most. Here the baby has lots of legs to lean on.

Elephants feel safest when they are near each other, and they do everything together.

The oldest and biggest female is the grandmother, and she is the leader of the Kichwa Tembo family. Because she has lived so long, she is also wise. She knows where to find the best food and water holes. She also decides when it's time for the family to move.

When elephants talk to each other, they make a strange rumbling noise in their throats.

The baby's father does not travel with the family. He moves around by himself or with other bulls in the area. The bulls spend their days wallowing, dusting, wrestling, and stuffing themselves with food. Each bull eats enough grass, roots and bark to fill a small truck.

Bull elephants have the largest tusks. They use their tusks to strip bark off trees, dig up juicy roots, and break off tasty branches. Sometimes the tusks are used to fight.

The baby elephant needs lots of attention. She stays close to her mother who, with her trunk, often strokes the infant. The caring mother uses her foot to lift the baby gently if she stumbles and falls. The baby elephant is still small enough to walk under her mother's belly and stand between her legs. Here the little one is safe from hungry lions and hyenas, which can sneak up in the tall grass.

Milk is the most important food for a baby elephant. When she is a few months old, she begins to chew on grass, soft leaves, and juicy roots. But she will continue to nurse until she is two years old. Like all babies, she plays with her food. Sometimes, she steals food from her mother's mouth to learn which foods are good to eat.

An elephant's trunk is handy. It's a nose, a trumpet, an arm, and a water pump all in one. The baby can use her trunk to toss a clump of grass, hug a cousin, grab her mother's tail, or scratch an itchy eye. But it takes practice. Sometimes, she even steps on her own trunk, and trips.

A trunk makes a perfect hose for spraying mud. When the family finds a gooey mud hole, they suck and squirt until everybody is slick and shiny. The wet mud cools them off. Then, once the mud dries, it protects their sensitive skin from the sun and biting insects, like the tsetse fly.

As the young elephant gets older and becomes a little braver, she spends more time away from her mother. She loves to play with her cousins. The playmates wrap their trunks together, push and tug, and chase each other around.

But the youngsters are not as brave as they seem. If a bird or rabbit suddenly flushes from the grass in front of them, the young elephants trumpet in fear and run to their mothers.

One day when the family is feeding in the marsh, they meet a herd of shaggy waterbucks. Even though water-bucks are not dangerous, when they are nearby, the elephants are nervous. But the baby elephant's big brother is not afraid of the waterbucks. He shakes his head, flaps his ears, and chases them away.

Because elephants are such large animals they need lots of space in which to live. Sometimes they must walk a long distance in a single day, crossing rivers and deep gullies. Long walks can be very tiring for a young elephant. A mother may need to push her baby up a hill with her trunk, or let the youngster hold on to her tail.

One day, after a long walk, the elephants are very thirsty.
The water hole has steep, slippery banks. When the family
stops to drink, the baby elephant gets trapped in the
hole. An aunt tries to lift the little one up with her trunk
but fails. Finally, the aunt wades into the water hole and
pushes the baby up to safety.

A baby elephant stays with its family for many years. When the young males become teenagers, they are chased away from the family and join other groups of males. But most young female elephants stay with the same family all of their lives. They help their mothers raise other babies until the young females are old enough to have babies of their own.

DID YOU KNOW?

- There are three kinds of elephants. The savanna elephant lives in eastern and southern Africa. The forest elephant lives in western and central Africa. And the Asian elephant lives in India and Southeast Asia.

- The savanna elephant is the largest land animal in the world. The largest bull ever measured was over thirteen feet (four meters) tall at its shoulders, and it weighed over twelve tons (twelve tonnes).

- An elephant can live almost as long as a human can. The oldest ever recorded was a female in captivity who was seventy-eight years old.

- Both male and female elephants have ivory tusks. The tusks first become visible when the young elephant is 2½ years old. By the time the animal is 6 years old, the tusks are almost 5 inches (12 centimeters) long. Bull elephants have the largest tusks. The longest pair ever measured was over 12 feet (3.4 meters) long. Together, the tusks weighed 293 pounds (133 kilograms).

- The number of calves a mother elephant will raise depends upon her nutrition. When food is plentiful, a female can have her first calf when she is thirteen years old, and then another calf every four years for most of her life. When food is scarce, she may have to wait as long as thirteen years to have another calf.

- Scientists recognize individual elephants by the shape of their tusks, the presence of scars and tears on the edge of their ears, and the pattern of blood vessels on the back of their ears.

- The mother elephant is pregnant for twenty-two months, longer than any other animal. This pregnancy is twice as long as the blue whale—the largest animal in the world.

INDEX

A
Africa, 7, 34
age, 34
appearance, 34
Asian elephants, 34

B
baby elephants,
    8, 16, 18, 34
birth, 8
bulls, 14, 34

C
calves, 34

F
families, 7, 10, 32
father elephants, 14
fear, 24, 26
feeding, 18
females, 32
fighting, 14
food, 18, 34
forest elephants, 34

G
grandmother
    elephants, 12
growing up, 24

K
kinds of elephants, 34

M
males, 32
milk, 18
mother, 8, 16, 18,
    28, 32
motherhood, 34
mud, 22

N
nursing, 18

P
play, 24
pregnancy, 34

S
safety, 10, 16
savanna elephants, 34
Serengeti Plains, 7
size, 34
space, 28

T
talking, 12
teenage elephants, 32
trunks, 20, 22
tusks, 14, 34

W
walking, 28
water hole, 30
waterbucks, 26
weight, 8, 34

BIOGRAPHIES

When Dr. Wayne Lynch met Aubrey Lang, he was an emergency doctor and she was a pediatric nurse. Within five years they were married and had left their jobs in medicine to work together as writers and wildlife photographers. For more than twenty years they have explored the great wilderness areas of the world—tropical rainforests, remote islands in the Arctic and Antarctic, deserts, mountains, and African grasslands.

Dr. Lynch is a popular guest lecturer and an award-winning science writer. He is the author of more than two dozen titles for adults and children. His books cover a wide range of subjects, from the biology and behavior of penguins and northern bears, arctic and grassland ecology, to the lives of prairie birds and mountain wildlife. He is a Fellow of the internationally recognized Explorers Club, and an elected Fellow of the prestigious Arctic Institute of North America.

Ms. Lang is the author of a dozen nature books for children. She loves to share her wildlife experiences with young readers, and has more stories to tell in the Nature Baby Series.

The couple's impressive photo credits include thousands of images published in over two dozen countries.

36

MTI